Bygone Troon

by Hugh Maxwell

Photographed around 1914 outside the boys' entrance to the Higher Grade School on Fullarton Street are men of the 3/1st Highland Divisional Signal Company of the Royal Engineers. Just visible at the bottom of the photograph is a number plate on a motorcycle, 'BS 115' denoting that the vehicle was registered and far travelled from the Orkney area. The man standing at the bottom left was the rider as he carried the initials DR (despatch rider) above the two chevrons denoting his rank of corporal.

Stenlake Publishing Ltd.

Text © Hugh Maxwell, 2018.
First published in the United Kingdom, 2018,
by Stenlake Publishing Ltd.,
54-58 Mill Square,
Catrine, Ayrshire,
KA5 6RD

Telephone: 01290 551122
www.stenlake.co.uk

ISBN 9781840337266

**The publishers regret that they cannot supply
copies of any pictures featured in this book.**

Acknowledgements

The author would like to thank the many Troonites who contributed information towards this book and also friends and family for their generous encouragement, support and assistance. The photograph on the front cover and page 31 is an ETW postcard.

Further Reading

The books listed below were used by the author during his research. None of them is available from Stenlake Publishing. Those interested in finding out more are advised to contact their local bookshop or reference library.

The Statistical Account of Scotland, 1791–1799.
The New Statistical Account of Scotland, 1845.
The Third Statistical Account of Scotland, 1951.
Ken Andrew, *Ayrshire Guide*, 1981.
Alan Godfrey, *Old Ordnance Survey Maps, Troon 1909*, 1988.
Dane Love, *Ayrshire – Discovering a County*, 2003.
George M'Michael, *Notes on the Way Through Ayrshire*, 1886.
Ian MacPherson, *Old Troon*, Stenlake Publishing, 2000.
John Strawhorn, *Ayrshire – The Story of a County*, 1975.
Stewart C. Wyllie and James Wilson, *Troon in Old Picture Postcards*, 1990.

The bustling Cross pictured around 1910. In his book *Notes on the Way Through Ayrshire: The Land of Burns, Wallace, Henry the Minstrel, and Covenant Martyrs'* (1886), George M'Michael described the town: 'Troon, the modern chief town of the parish, is… built on a plan partly rectangular and partly crescent, suiting the circle of the south sands, and contains a number of handsome streets, with numerous neatly built villas and cottages, garnished with flower and other gardens, and is a healthy resort for sea bathers.'

Introduction

Established on a small headland with sandy beaches to both the north and south, Troon is believed to take its name from the Gaelic *An t Sron* which translates as 'the nose' or 'the bill', a fairly accurate description of its location on a jutting promontory on the shores of the Firth of Clyde, eight miles to the north of Ayr and six miles to the south of Irvine.

In 1344 King Robert II granted a charter to the Fullarton family of Ayrshire, giving them ownership of the lands of Crosbie, Lady Isle and Orangefield. The Fullartons built Crosbie Tower house about one and a half miles south-east of Troon. This had a vaulted basement containing a dungeon and from this house they administered justice and oversaw their estate.

The earliest records of Troon date from around this time and describe it as containing just a few scattered small cottages along or near the shore with a small inn and most of the inhabitants engaged in fishing, farming and panning salt from the sea water.

By the seventeenth century Troon, still of very little significance, was now within Dundonald Parish with the village of Dundonald being the principle trading centre. Throughout this century and well into the eighteenth the smuggling trade went on along the entire Ayrshire coast with contraband goods such as brandy, tea, tobacco, rum, fine silk and linens being brought ashore illegally under cover of darkness. Troon was described at this time as being a being a bare rocky peninsula running out from a dreary waste of sand and grass, inhabited by only a few fisher folk who dwelt in miserable huts. It was, however, perfect for the contraband trade and many cargoes brought from the Isle of Man were smuggled ashore from the luggers hovering offshore. The contraband goods would than be secretly transported to nearby towns and cities and sold there without any duties being paid.

Around 1668 an attempt was made by an enterprising company of merchants to transform the natural headland into the principle port of Glasgow, but this failed when an attempt to secure sufficient ground in the vicinity was unsuccessful. The merchants then chose an alternative, less-favourable site which later became Port Glasgow.

Due to its location on the coast Troon farmers had traditionally gathered seaweed from the shore to spread across their fields as an early type of fertiliser. In the first half of the eighteenth century William Fullarton had tried to encourage this industry on his estate by constructing a small works for the drying and burning of seaweed, the ash being rich in potash and soda, but this was only partly successful.

In 1707 a royal charter was granted to Fullarton to form a free port at Troon (meaning traders and merchants could trade freely) and to charge a levy on any vessel that dropped anchor to load and unload goods. No evidence exists to show that the charter was ever implemented to any great extent and it would not be until a hundred and forty years later that the third Duke of Portland, who had become the proprietor of the lands of Fullarton in 1805, used his wealth and influence to take important steps towards developing Troon into a commercial port.

By the 1790s large scale mining of coal and other minerals was being undertaken south of Kilmarnock on the Caprington Estate with all the coal being exported overseas to Ireland through the port at Irvine. Around this time Ayrshire badly needed a harbour that could handle larger ships to help further exploit the mining industry and make it more profitable. By 1808, exploiting the natural harbour that existed, the east pier, west pier, wet dock, graving docks, storehouses and offices were all built. The harbour was also dredged and deepened to accommodate ships over 250 tons. This cost more than £100,000 but quickly encouraged trade and industry and transformed Troon into Ayrshire's main coal port. Finally, the hamlet of a few scattered rundown cottages began to change and prosper. Increased activity along the coast by the Admiralty and more favourable taxes on certain goods also saw smuggling steadily decline while the port rapidly became a centre for fishing, trade and the export of goods and minerals.

In 1812 the Duke of Portland, one of Ayrshire's wealthiest landowners, opened the first industrial railway in Scotland, the nine-and-a-half-mile line which was used to transport coal from his mines at Kilmarnock to the port at Troon. Wagons, loaded with up to twelve tons of coal and other minerals, were initially horse drawn but in 1817 one of the first steam locomotive engines, 'The Duke' designed by George Stephenson, was used for a short period. However, it was both too heavy, breaking the iron rails, and too slow, drawing only ten-ton wagons at a slower speed of just five miles per hour, but a hugely important innovation nonetheless. The line would later convert to steam using more suitable locomotives and by the middle of the century over 170,000 tons of coal per year were being conveyed to Troon for export, principally to Ireland. The line also started carrying passengers.

The duke established shipbuilding at Troon in 1815 and by 1843 the yard was leased to the Troon Shipbuilding Company. With its two dry docks, the yard gained a reputation for building the finest vessels and this continued until 1885 when the Ailsa Ship Building Company – named after a founding partner, the third Marquess of Ailsa – took over. Meanwhile, the ballast bank was constructed around the mid 1860s from the rocks left over from the excavation of the harbour and the excess ballast used by the vessels transporting the coal. It provided further shelter from the strong south westerly winds and offered a safe anchorage to larger vessels using the harbour.

In 1840 the Glasgow & South Western Railway Company opened its passenger station to the east of the town, providing a direct link with Glasgow and bringing thousands of holidaymakers during the summer. Troon flourished, the population climbing to 2,300. In 1892 a loop line was constructed along with a new railway station which brought passengers directly into the centre of the town. The harbour was purchased from the Duke of Portland by the railway company in 1901 and it ran trains down to the coast to meet the pleasure cruises run by its fleet of steamers. Troon's other holiday attractions were tennis courts, bowling greens, boating around the bay, donkey rides along the beach, and its numerous cafes, restaurants and gift shops. Several large hotels opened and there were many boarding houses. Golf also grew in popularity and several planned courses were constructed.

Land was made available in the form of feus by the Duke of Portland's Commissioner from 1810 onwards to enable the building of houses. Building was purposefully planned around the two important areas of the harbour and the Cross. In 1896 Troon achieved burgh status; meanwhile the population increased to over 5,000. Demolition of some of older buildings began and these were replaced by buildings of more prominence and grandeur such as the Unionist Hall Buildings at Templehill and the commercial buildings along Ayr Street.

Into the twentieth century, Troon continued to grow. Between 1919 and 1948 over four hundred private houses were built as well as a large number of council houses. The population by 1950 was 10,000 but by this time there was also decline as the Barassie Carriage and Wagon Works ceased building wagons and became only a repair yard before eventually closing in 1973. Shipbuilding also declined but was partly offset by the increase in ship breaking of former wartime and navy vessels at the British Iron and Steel Corporation yard. The coal and mineral trade had virtually ceased by the 1950s, while passenger numbers on the pleasure steamers also gradually dwindled. Holidaymakers began to be enticed away from traditional destinations to locations abroad and local hotels and boarding houses catered more for day trippers or those staying for perhaps only a weekend instead of a week or longer.

Despite these economic changes, throughout the twentieth century the town continued to expand and by 1974 the population was 11,000. That year saw local government reorganisation with Troon losing its independent burgh status and becoming incorporated into the much larger Kyle and Carrick District Council.

Since then, shipbuilding has ceased although boats are still maintained and repaired at the harbour and the inner harbour has been transformed into a bustling marina. In 1999 a regular SeaCat catamaran ferry service was introduced, linking Troon to Larne. This was discontinued in 2016 although a freight service still operates. The harbour is now operated by Associated British Ports and frequently handles larger fishing and cargo vessels as well as thousands of logs which are brought here annually from the forests of Cowal and Argyll. They are stored at the harbour side and processed at the nearby computer-controlled sawmill which is still operated by Adam Wilson and Sons. The saw mill has expanded over the years to become one of the largest in the country, producing softwood products for the construction, fencing, pallet and packaging markets.

Golf is now the chief tourist attraction, with golfers from all over the world visiting to play on the town's five courses. The Royal Troon Golf Club has hosted the Open Championship nine times, most recently in 2016 when it attracted over 170,000 visitors. Troon is now part of the South Ayrshire council area and the population stands at around 14,500. With its excellent transport links to Glasgow and the central belt many people travel to work further afield and the town remains a very

A view of the Cross from around 1880. The steeple of the Old Parish Church, built in 1838, towers above the houses in the background. On the left are the two-storey buildings at the corner of Ayr Street, with Cunningham's Public House, on the corner which were later replaced with the tenement of 1902/03. Apart from this the view is instantly recognisable today with only the shops and their owners having changed.

Ayr Street, viewed from the junction with Academy Street and looking towards the Cross, 1902. The new parish church was designed by Hippolyte J. Blanc and the inaugural stone was laid on 28 October 1893 by the Duke and Duchess of Portland. They had travelled down from Fullarton House in miserable conditions but despite the wet and windy weather a large crowd had gathered for the occasion. The new church opened on 26 December 1895. It was always the intention to put another towering steeple, planned to be 180 feet in height, atop the square tower visible on the left here, but this was never completed as it was felt by many to be an unnecessary cost and would ultimately spoil the look of this beautiful building. The steeple on the old church was also deemed sufficient.

Looking westwards from the Cross into Templehill around 1909. The Union Bank had previously been located near the top of Templehill but relocated to the Unionist Club Buildings when they were completed in 1894. Across the road are the premises of Shaw's bakery and further along the street, just to the right of the gas lamp, is the single-storey building occupied by the Ailsa Bar, later the premises of Tog's Café. For many years the Bank of Scotland occupied the former premises of the Union Bank, although these closed in October 2017.

A large crowd of spectators lines the bottom of Templehill and the Cross on a wet day eagerly awaiting some sort of procession, perhaps marking the Diamond Jubilee of Queen Victoria in 1897 or the Coronation of King Edward VII in 1901. Dominating the street are the Unionist Club Buildings and Hall, built in 1894/95.

Looking down Templehill, c. 1915, towards the four-storey tenement built in 1902/03 at the corner of Portland Street and Ayr Street. Templehill took its name from a 'folly' or 'Temple' that was built in this area by Colonel William Fullarton in the eighteenth century when he owned nearby Fullarton Estate. It was an octagonal shaped building with a domed roof supported by eight stone pillars, used by the family as a resting place when out for a walk. Being located near the top of the hill, it commanded excellent views. Locals often referred to it as 'Fullarton's Folly' but no trace remains. Little has changed in this view; only the large paved area on the right has disappeared to make way for car parking.

The top of Templehill in the early 1900s, viewed from the Harbour Road. On the right is the Co-operative shop whilst on the left, second after the lamp post, is the premises of the Knowe Hotel and Harbour Bar. On the extreme left is the gable of the Union Bank of Scotland building and just out of view next to this was Troon's oldest hotel, the Portland Arms Hotel. Dating from 1812, this hotel was built by the Duke of Portland adjacent the terminus for the Troon to Kilmarnock railway. Originally it had been used as a stopping point for the horse drawn stagecoaches which brought passengers from the first railway station. Today the Portland Arms has been renamed the Anchorage Hotel and it remains popular, as does the Harbour Bar.

Located at the top of Templehill was the small walled garden known locally as 'Morney's Park'. Pictured here in March 1924, it was donated by Adam Wood, a shipyard manager who owned nearby Portland Villa further along the street. On the right is the three-storey Exchange Building that served as the shipping office for the port until it was demolished in 1938. The garden area still exists today, although without the flagpole, and overlooks the marina in the inner harbour.

The Miner's Welfare Home was located at the top of Templehill on Wood Road in a large house formerly known as Portland Villa. The house dated from around the 1840s and had been owned by the shipyard manager named Adam Wood until 1924 when it was acquired by the District Welfare Committee of the Ayrshire Coal-owners' Association and of the Ayrshire Miners' Union. In 1936 the villa was converted into a convalescent home for the use of miners' wives and their daughters, with men staying at Kirkmichael House near Maybole. Following the closure of Kirkmichael House in 1956, men were also accommodated into the home at Troon.

A view of the grounds of the Miners' Home, c. 1938. The home closed in the 1990s and the building was subsequently demolished. The area of the house and gardens has now been extensively redeveloped with many residential private houses being built along Wood Road, Wood Court and Bradan Road.

A view of the Miners' Welfare Home with its gardens, taken around 1960.

The grounds of the Miner's Welfare Home pictured in the early 1940s. In the foreground is one of the croquet lawns and the summer house is also visible in the centre of the garden. On the left are the then-new council houses on Wood Road, while on the right are the gardens and rear of the council houses that were built on Welbeck Crescent. The home closed temporarily in 1984 as a result of the miners' strike. It reopened later and finally closed in the 1990s.

An early 1900s view of Troon Harbour from the top of Templehill, with carriages loaded with coal in the foreground waiting to be shunted down to the outer harbour and loaded onto a vessel. The inner harbour was being used for logging and the storage of logs at this time and in the background are the buildings of the Ailsa Shipbuilding Yard next to the graving docks. This scene has changed greatly today with the modern marina now occupying this area and the railway line and ground on the right given over to car parking.

The inner harbour at Troon in 1908 with the East Pier on the right and the railway line that ran along it also visible. On the left are the buildings of the Ailsa Shipbuilding Yard. Out of view on the left were the buildings, cranes and timber yard of the Harbour Saw Mill, founded in 1870 and located near the Titchfield Cottages. The saw mill is operated by Adam Wilson and Sons Ltd and is one of the largest sawmills in the UK, employing over 100 people.

Men hard at work caulking the hull of the *Wildwood* in the graving dock in the early 1890s. The *Wildwood* was a large barque built in 1883 by Joseph K. Dunlop at Saint John, New Brunswick, Canada, where the vessel was also registered. The vessel was used principally for transporting timber and other goods between Canada and Scotland. Near the end of her career she was converted to a barge for the transport of gypsum from the mines near the Avon River in Nova Scotia to New York. The *Wildwood* was then deliberately beached in January 1923 at Summerville, Nova Scotia, and set alight with three other vessels, presumably a cost-effective way of disposing of them when they finished service. The graving dock was located off the outer harbour (there was another one adjacent the wet dock in the outer harbour). Caulking was the practice of driving oakum, cotton or rope fibres into the seams of a wooden ship's hull to make it watertight and also restrict the movement of any planks.

The three-masted barque *Dalhanna*, built in Glasgow in 1881, photographed while at Troon Harbour for repairs to extensive damage caused by a fierce storm. On 12 February 1896 the inhabitants of Troon were startled by the noise and shockwaves of a tremendous explosion. Houses along the South Beach were shaken so violently glass was smashed and doors and windows rattled. Suffering from storm damage, the schooner *Secret* from St Ives in Cornwall had drifted onto the Black Rocks, about two miles south of Troon Harbour. Her cargo consisted of fifteen tons of dynamite and blasting gelatines and this had suddenly exploded although fortunately after the crew had succeeded in abandoning ship and getting ashore. Witnesses saw a huge column of water rise to a towering height, crowned with a cloud of thick smoke; the noise of the explosion was even heard many miles inland. The schooner was totally blown to pieces and a case of dynamite was later found on the beach among the washed up wreckage by a number of local boys. To prevent any further disasters from occurring, the shore was patrolled for days afterwards by the local constabulary.

The Ailsa Shipbuilding Company built many vessels, including SS *Wollongbar* seen here being launched from yard 229 in 1911. The steam ship was built for the North Coast Steam Navigation Company which was registered in Sydney, Australia. She was one of the fastest vessels on the Australian Coast at the time but did not last long as she was blown ashore and wrecked in bad weather at Byron Bay, New South Wales, in 1921. The vessel was subsequently broken up and dismantled *in situ* at Byron Bay.

The three-masted steel barque *Killoran* was built in 1900 by the Ailsa Shipbuilding Co. Ltd at yard No. 88 for James Browne, founder of the Killoran Barque Company Ltd of Glasgow. The sailing vessel was launched on 30 June 1900 and was over 260 feet in length. *Killoran* was used for a time for the transport of grain, other cargoes, and passengers between San Francisco and Europe. She was sold to J. Hardie and Co. of Glasgow in 1909 and then in 1924 to a Finnish owner, Gustav Erikson of Mariehamn. The barque then operated from this port in the Baltic Sea. *Killoran* was recorded as having journeys to Australia and New Zealand. On 15 August 1940 she was stopped by a German auxiliary cruiser and sunk by explosives 400 miles south west of the Azores. Despite the vessel having Finnish owners the Germans believed she was sailing under British orders at the time, hence the sinking. This photograph from the 1930s shows the vessel leaving port and flying the Finnish flag.

A group of apprentice platers employed by the Ailsa Shipbuilding Company, pictured at the harbour in 1921. In the background is one of the cranes that were used to move large steel plates into position when building a ship in the graving dock. There were two graving docks and also a large wet dock at the Ailsa Yard and in 1975 a large covered berth was also constructed. Many types of vessels including ferries, frigates, patrol boats, mine sweepers, cargo and passenger ships were constructed over the years and the yard also undertook conversion, repair, overhaul and fabrication work. Following nationalisation in 1977 it was nationalised and subsumed into the British Shipbuilders Corporation and in 1986, after being privatised, it was acquired by the Perth Corporation and renamed the Ailsa & Perth Ltd. Large-scale ship building ceased at Troon in 1988 and the yard closed in 2000, although some smaller vessels have been repaired there since.

Passengers boarding the *Juno*, c. 1906, with the *Troon* passing by. The tug was built by J.P. Rennoldson and Sons, South Shields, and after her service at Troon was purchased by the Middlesbrough Towage Company in 1930, serving on the River Tyne until February 1948 when she sank while moored at Morpeth Dock after metal thieves stole piping, resulting in her taking on water. The *Troon* was salvaged a few months later and that same year was sold for scrap to the British Iron and Steel Company and subsequently broken up at their yard in Tranmere.

The steam paddle-tug *Walney* was built in 1904 by J.P. Rennoldson and Sons of South Shields for the Furness Railway Company in Barrow. She was later adapted to carry 100 passengers in her fore saloon for excursion work between Barrow and Fleetwood. *Walney* was owned by a number of different companies during her long lifespan including the British Transport Docks Board and the London Midland and Scottish Railway Company for whom she operated as a tug for many years, principally between Troon and Ayr. In November 1952 she was broken up at Troon; this photograph shows her moored in the outer harbour.

Pictured leaving the harbour is the steel screw cargo steamer, the *Skeldon,* which was built in 1903 by the Ailsa Shipbuilding Company Ltd in Yard 115 at Troon. Registered in Belfast and owned by the Shamrock Shipping Company Ltd based in Larne Harbour, the *Skeldon* was wrecked on 1 June 1934 when she ran aground onto the rocks of Des Porles Shoal near Jardin Light, France, and broke in two. She was carrying a load of coal from Port Talbot in Wales to St Malo in Brittany and the wreck can still be seen on the site today.

A view of the outer harbour from the East Pier, c. 1915. The *Troon* is pulling the *Matienzo* towards her mooring posts and the unloading cranes near the wet dock, just out of view on the right. The *Matienzo* was a steel screw steamer built in 1899 by Robert Thompson and Sons at the Southwick Yard and Bridge Dockyard, Sunderland. The vessel was later sold and renamed the *Begona No. 3* and later the *Zurriola*, but continued to operate as a general cargo ship until she was eventually broken up for scrap at Valencia, Spain, in May 1964.

The S.S. *Juno* pictured around 1903 with passengers embarking near the end of the West Pier. Visible on the left are two of the large stationery cranes and also one of the mobile cranes that ran on the rail tracks alongside the pier. The crane in the distance was steam operated. Inside was a fire that was stoked by the operator to heat up the water in the boiler to power the crane. Dating from the late 1800s, it remained in use until sometime into the 1960s before being dismantled.

The paddle steamer *Juno* at the outer harbour, *c.* 1911. On the left are the large cranes that were used to load and unload cargo from ships while on the right is the lighthouse at the end of the west pier. The *Juno* had operated from Ayr since 1898 and was a regular sight on the Firth of Clyde until she was taken out of service and scrapped at Alloa in 1932. Many other vessels called at Troon when offering their 'Pleasure Excursions'; from the 1930s these included the turbine steamer *The Duchess of Hamilton* which would also call at Ayr, Ardrossan, Girvan, Millport, Largs and Arran and was operated by the London Midland and Scottish Railway Company and the Caledonian Steam Packet Company Ltd.

Following the outbreak of the First World War the *Juno* was requisitioned by the Admiralty and, renamed HMS *Junior*, was used as a minesweeper in the firths of Clyde and Forth. Following the end of hostilities the *Juno* operated on the Rothesay run for a while but returned to Ayr in 1919 and was again used predominantly for excursions until she was sold in 1931 and broken up for scrap the following year at Alloa Docks.

The P.S. *Juno* leaving Troon Harbour in 1910. The small lighthouse on the end of the West Pier is on the left. The *Juno* was a 600-ton paddle steamer built in 1898 by the Clydebank Engineering and Shipbuilding Company for the Glasgow & South Western Railway Company. The vessel operated from Ayr and was used for excursions to Arran and many other popular destinations besides Troon, such as Millport, Largs, Arrochar, Lochgoilhead and Inveraray.

This photograph from the East Pier shows the small draw bridge that allowed access to and from the inner harbour. In the background are some of the cranes that were used to load and unload coal and goods that were shipped through the port. In 1871, at the request of the inhabitants, Troon lifeboat station was built on Portland Street at a cost of £250. It was equipped with a 32-foot rowing boat which was pulled on a wooden carriage down to the shore before being launched into the sea. A crew had been established the previous year and it was not until 1905 that it was deemed necessary to have the boat afloat at all times to quicken rescue times. The lifeboat house was sold and the boat was moored down at the harbourside; in November 1929 a motor boat was brought into service. In 1987 a boathouse was built near the wet dock and this was extended in 1996; two vessels – the Trent Class all-weather RNLB *Jim Moffat* and the D-Class inshore lifeboat D-684 *Telford Shopping Centre* – are now stationed here. Three medals have been awarded for bravery to crew members and the RNLI also have a shop on Ayr Street.

A view of the outer harbour in the early 1920s with one of the large cranes that ran on rails either side of the rail tracks in the foreground. The iron paddle tug *Troon* can be seen moored alongside the East Pier with a number of cranes and coal wagons on the sidings in the background. The initials G&SW are visible on the side of one of the wagons; in 1901 the Duke of Portland sold the harbour to the Glasgow & South Western Railway Company. Ship breaking started at Troon in 1903 and was undertaken by the West of Scotland Shipbreaking Co. Ltd which broke up for scrap over 440 vessels of all types and sizes, many naval including submarines. Three or four vessels could be seen at any one time moored on this pier in various stages of the breaking process. Larger hulks were often tied up on the north side of the breakwater and vessels were frequently hauled up and beached at low tide in the inner harbour. Ship breaking ceased in the late 1980s.

Three puffers and a fishing boat pictured in the wet dock in 1958. On the left is the *Texan*, built in 1937, and next to her is the *Spartan*, built in 1942 by J. Hay & Sons, Kirkintilloch, and one of only two surviving Scottish built 'puffers'. After a hard working career she was acquired by the Scottish Maritime Museum, Irvine, being the first vessel in their collection in 1983. At the museum the *Spartan* is on display to the public, restored to full working order and painted in its original black and red livery. In the background is the *Sealight* built in 1930 at Greenock.

Pierrots performing near the south end of the Ballast Bank around 1910. Known as 'Dad Lindsay's Pierrots', the five members of this troop performed outdoors twice daily at 11 a.m. and also at 3.30 p.m., weather permitting, during the summer months. In the evenings they were regular performers to much larger audiences in the Concert Hall and also entertained smaller groups who hired them for private parties. This photograph also shows the small stage that was used with the flat ground visible in the background that led to the inner harbour. Today this area is now occupied by the council houses of Titchfield Road, Ailsa Road and Harbour Road, and the site where the Pierrots performed is now a small play park.

The south end of the Ballast Bank at Troon in 1921. This was constructed from around the 1840s onwards by the Duke of Portland to protect the harbour and its entrance from the strong south westerly gales that often damaged shipping attempting to enter the narrow harbour. Rock excavated from the construction of the harbour and the wet dock was used in its construction, along with the excess ballast from cargo and freight vessels that visited the harbour. This built up the protection offered to the harbour by the natural headland that already existed. Today the Ballast Bank provides one of the finest elevated views over Troon and also out across the Firth of Clyde to the Lady Isle. This photograph shows some children fishing in the tidal pools at the area known as Port Ronnald with the masts of a ship at the harbour visible in the background.

Looking down onto Titchfield Road from the slightly elevated height of the Ballast Bank around 1936. On the left is the junction for Wood Road, followed by the extensive gardens and grounds of the Miner's Convalescent Home, and then the junction of the street that was originally known as Back Templehill. Further along is the distinctive bowed frontage of Pladda View. The flats of Wood Court now occupy the former grounds of the Miner's Convalescent Home.

This photograph from the early 1900s shows Pladda View on Titchfield Road, overlooking the shore with the houses on Welbeck Crescent visible to the left. The houses take their name from the small uninhabited island of Pladda which is located at the southern tip of the Isle of Arran and is often visible on a clear day.

A 1912 view looking eastwards along Welbeck Crescent towards the junction with West Portland Street. Visible in the centre distance is the spire of the original Old Parish Church with the new church adjacent to the right. The central spire of the newer church can be seen; it was removed in 1975 after it was found to be unsafe due to weather damage. The large tower spire originally planned for it was never built.

Looking westwards along Welbeck Crescent in the early 1920s, with the street curving round to the left to join Titchfield Road at the shore. The motor car in the view carries the initials 'GA' on its number plate which denotes that it was registered in Glasgow in 1921/22. Welbeck Crescent was named after the Duke of Portland's family seat of Welbeck Abbey in Nottinghamshire.

Looking northwards towards the then-new bandstand and beyond, *c.* 1906. The Esplanade can be seen curving round the bay with the houses on Portland Terrace and Titchfield Road in the background. On 29 December 1894, the *Frey*, a Norwegian ship sailing from America bound for Greenock with a cargo of pitch pine, was dashed against these offshore rocks. The vessel had dropped her anchors between the Lady Isle and Troon Harbour during a gale, but the wind increased in ferocity to hurricane strength. Rockets were launched for help as the *Frey* was forced onto the rocks near the shore and by daybreak extensive damage had been done to her masts and rigging. The Troon lifeboat was launched but it proved impossible to get beyond the harbour wall due to the strength of the gale and the Irvine lifeboat was summoned. Huge crowds gathered along the shore to watch the rescue of the sixteen crew members but when all were safely aboard the Irvine lifeboat it was then struck by a towering wave and overturned, throwing everyone overboard. Men were seen clinging desperately to the lifelines and luckily all were able to either swim ashore or were rescued, apart from the ship's steward who, unable to swim, drowned in the stormy seas.

A storm hits the Esplanade in 1911. In January 1884, Troon, along with the rest of the British Isles, experienced one of the worst storms recorded, which raged for over three weeks. Serious flooding occurred and 110 yards of railway line along the coast was completely destroyed; in some cases the force of the water washed the sleepers away.

On 26 November 1912 a severe south-westerly storm hit the west of Scotland, resulting in the deaths of ten people. Terrible flooding occurred at many coastal towns including Largs, Irvine and Troon which experienced the worst flooding recorded in the town's history. Due to the ferocity of the gale towering waves crashed ashore and, combined with a high tide, the water was unable to drain away due to the relentless strength of the wind. Considerable damage was done to many properties in and around the Cross area where the water reached a depth of up to four feet and inhabitants were fearful for both their properties and their lives. This is the view of the flood waters at the Cross area, looking along Templehill towards the harbour.

This view shows the flood on Portland Street with Welsh's grocer's shop being inundated on the corner. Such was the impact of the gales on 26 November that the Higher Grade School closed at noon with all the pupils being sent home for their own safety. However, such was the speed of the flood that many children couldn't get home and had to stay with friends or relatives. After the flood the Burgh Council took action and the ground near the top of the Esplanade overlooking Portland Terrace, where most of the water had come from, was eventually raised in height. This helped to prevent and protect the town from the worst of later storms though flooding to some extent has occurred since.

The flood waters on Ayr Street, looking towards the Cross, with the premises of A. Sherriff's chemist visible on the right at Nos. 19/21. During the storm the 'sea rose higher and higher' before spilling into the town over the esplanade wall with catastrophic results. Portland and West Portland Street were totally flooded as were the Cross and Ayr Street along with Templehill, the Old Parish Church, Welbeck Crescent, Church Street, Barassie Street, Union Street and the houses on Harbour Row. Winds in excess of seventy miles per hour were recorded at the height of the storm and destruction occurred in all parts of the town, including the harbour where moored vessels were battered by the wind and several ships were driven onto the sands of the North Shore at Barassie. After the storm subsided a considerable area of the road and grassy area just to the south of the Ballast Bank facing Titchfield Road was found to have been washed away. Large sections of the sea wall that ran alongside the Esplanade on the South Beach had also been broken up, washed away or severely damaged.

The Esplanade c. 1913 with the bandstand visible in the background along with the houses on Portland Terrace and Titchfield Road. Many of the streets in Troon were named after the town's most important and influential benefactor, William Henry Bentinck, fourth Duke of Portland and Marquess of Titchfield, who lived nearby at Fullarton House. They included Portland Terrace and Portland Street, Welbeck Crescent after the family's ancestral seat, Welbeck Abbey in Nottinghamshire, and also Bentinck Drive and Titchfield Road.

The Bathing Station at Troon was located on the rocks near the end of Welbeck Crescent in an area known as Betsy's Kirn In this photograph from the 1930s a bather can be seen jumping into the sea from the springboard that was bolted onto the edge of the rocks. The metal railings to the side helped bathers to pull themselves out of the water whilst on the far right is the small changing shelter with its round lifebuoy. Even after the purpose-built swimming pond was opened nearby in 1931, sea bathing remained popular here up until the 1950s.

The swimming pond and car park were opened just off Titchfield Road in 1931 and are pictured here around 1938. The heated pond had purpose-built changing rooms and elevated spectator areas overlooking it. From the 1970s dwindling visitor numbers, combined with the lack of a roof to protect swimmers and spectators from the elements, saw the pond gradually fall into disrepair. Later, an indoor heated pool was opened nearby and the swimming pond was finally demolished in 1987, with part of the area now being used as a public car park.

A corner of the swimming pond in the early 1940s. Every year it was open from June through to August.

A race at the swimming pond in 1932. The photograph also shows the large chute which was very popular. The shallow end of the pond was near the main entrance, with the deeper end next to the sea. During the Second World War the pond may have been used by the Commandos for training purposes.

The swimming pond and the Italian rock garden, pictured in the early 1930s. The letters were painted onto the Esplanade wall so they would be visible to holidaymakers along the beach. While the pond has long since closed, the rock gardens still remain.

A view looking northeast along Titchfield Road in the late 1920s. In the background are the houses on Portland Terrace and the Esplanade is visible curving round the bay to the right past the houses on St Clair Terrace, with the spires of the old and new parish churches in the background. Notice how the grassy area appears to have been increased in height in front of the houses in an attempt to create flood barriers.

The shelter and bandstand near the top of the Esplanade in October 1914. Behind the shelter is the small drinking fountain which was presented to the town by James Dickie in 1891. On the far right are some of the boats that could be hired by holidaymakers to row around the bay. This scene has now changed greatly with the building of the Municipal Buildings in the area behind the bandstand.

The rowing boats were always very popular and were hired out to holidaymakers by retired sailors during the summer season as a source of income. The boat hirers often had small wooden huts on the beach and for a small fee anyone could spend an hour or so rowing around the bay, enjoying the splendid views and the peace and quiet away from the crowded beach. Regular boat trips were also organised from the harbour out to and around the Lady Isle.

Troon Burgh Military Band performing at the bandstand in 1910. The bandstand was built in 1906 and was a popular facility until the opening of the nearby Municipal Building and Concert Hall in 1932 saw it fall into disuse and disrepair. It was finally demolished in 1959 and replaced by a boating and paddling pond. The nearby shelter seen in the previous photograph was also removed.

These young children are certainly 'having a good time' paddling in the sea off the South Beach in 1908.

A beach scene from around 1910. The donkey rides and the rowing boats were among the town's main attractions and helped transform it into a bustling coastal resort during the summer months.

Enjoying the golden sunlit sands at Troon c. 1910, a young lad is hard at work building his sandcastle. The private residence of Marine Cottage on Academy Street is visible in the centre of this view. It was demolished in the early 1970s and luxury flats named Marine View Court now occupy the site.

'The Monte Carlo Rally' funfair ride on the Esplanade in the early 1970s. Visible in the background on the left is the public car park and the Portland Parish Church whilst in the centre are the public toilets and South Beach kiosk. At this time Troon was still a busy holiday destination on the coast but on fine summer days it also attracted large numbers of day trippers. The message on the reverse of this postcard reads: 'To John, having a great time. Weather is lovely. Now looking forward to seeing you again.' The funfair has long since been replaced with a children's playground and a crazy golf course.

The paddling pool and boating pond was built along the seafront following the demolition of the ornamental bandstand in 1959. Today, the shelter on the right still exists as does the paddling pool although it is now little used, while further along the Esplanade is a relatively recent crazy golf course and also a large play park.

The Concert Hall on South Beach viewed in 1947 from the Esplanade with Academy Street in the foreground. The Municipal Buildings were built in 1932 from a neo-Georgian design by James Miller. The two-storey-with-attic building was constructed from red brick with sandstone facings and given a distinctive red tile roof. The main entrance faces onto South Beach with steps leading up to a columned entrance with a small balcony above the door and crowning balustrade along the roof. The Concert Hall's stage has been graced with many famous Scottish entertainers over the years and has also been the venue for innumerable dances, concerts and plays.

The Beach Pavilion and the Town Hall, viewed in 1937 from the Esplanade with the Old Parish Church visible on the left. This view shows the entrance to the Concert Hall at the Municipal Buildings and on the right is a sign advertising the tearoom that was popular with holidaymakers at this time. This view has now changed with the addition, on the right, of the adjoining Walker Halls in 1974/75. The site of the Municipal Buildings had been gifted to the burgh by Sir Alexander Walker who also contributed considerable funds towards their construction cost. Famous for his blended whisky, Johnnie Walker, Sir Alexander Walker resided nearby at Piersland Lodge, which was built in 1899.

Looking south along the Esplanade with the war memorial visible on the left. This was designed by Alfred Gilbert from Birmingham and erected in 1924.

The sands and Esplanade in the mid 1930s. On the left is the small white hut at the bottom of St Meddans Street where deck chairs could be hired. Adjacent is another wooden hut that would have been used by one of the ice cream vendors at this time such as Giovanni Togneri. He had arrived at Troon from Tuscany and established his business in 1901, initially selling ice creams and refreshments from a cart although he later built a wooden café at Templehill. This burned down and he moved a couple of doors down to the site of the former Ailsa Bar in 1914 but during the summer months also sold his products from one of the wooden huts at the Sands. Tog's Café was later run by his son and it became one of the most famous Italian cafes on the west coast. It was located at No. 9 Templehill next to Macintyre's Bar and many people will still remember with great fondness the original glass frontage and the green and black vitreous marble counter. The café closed in August 2005.

In the 1930s Troon was often described as the 'Ideal Summer Holiday Resort' on colourful railway posters which were prominently displayed at station platforms across Scotland and England. Its attractions were 'six golf courses, a large sandy beach, boating, bathing, tennis, bowling … and other attractions'. The posters also stated that 'The golf courses on the west coast of Scotland are most conveniently reached by the Midland and Glasgow & South Western Railways.' The other attractions must have been the numerous beach cafes, the gift shops, three large cinemas, the newly built Beach Pavilion and Concert Hall, the putting green, donkey rides and regular steamship excursions from the harbour to the other resorts on the Clyde.

Another busy scene at the South Beach in the late 1930s, with holidaymakers sitting on their deck chairs enjoying the seaside weather which, on this day at least, obviously required the wearing of hats and coats.

A view of the sandy beach on what appears to be a beautiful summer's day in the 1940s. Visible on the shoreline on the right are the wooden plank ways that allowed access out onto the water and the rowing boats that could be hired.

Sadly the donkey rides which were a traditional and iconic attraction for many years at the seaside have long disappeared at Troon.

The Boating Stance, Troon.

In this view one of the boat hirers can be seen standing on the wooden plank way while in the background another has waded out into the water near the boats. Meanwhile, in the foreground two boys are ready to launch their own wooden boat into the sea.

The South Beach, 1924. These bathing huts were pulled down to the water's edge by horses and were available to hire for a small hourly fee. With the opening of the heated swimming pond in 1931, less people bathed directly in the sea and sadly the huts had disappeared from the shoreline by the 1950s.

Another view of the bathing huts from the 1920s, a time when sea bathing was seen as offering many recuperative and therapeutic benefits and was recommended along with the ingestion of sea water. In those days it was not uncommon to see people bathe in the sea even during the autumn and winter months.

The putting green was located on the flat grassy foreshore area just south of Victoria Drive, sandwiched between the Esplanade and the gardens to the rear of the houses on South Beach. In this view from March 1924 the Esplanade is visible on the right.

This photograph from around 1910 shows the Troon Co-operative Society bakery van opposite the Co-op Dairy which stood in Portland Street beside the Masonic Lodge. The Co-operative Society also had a shop opposite the harbour at Templehill. The roundsman can be seen atop his van and his job was to load up the carriage first thing in the morning and then go round the streets selling fresh bakery produce. He was also responsible for the welfare and upkeep of the horse.

Scottish Transport ran a regular bus from Troon to Dundonald and then onto Kilmarnock and it is seen here in the early 1920s parked in front of the houses at the bottom of West Portland Street, opposite the Dickie Drinking Fountain. The bus is a Leyland and carries the Lanarkshire registration of VA 2301 which was used from July 1922 until July 1930. Wooden destination and route boards are visible at the front and along the side of the bus and these had to be turned over manually once the bus had reached the terminus. Noticeable is the solid rubber tyres which must have made for a very bumpy ride for the passengers and on the front of the bus is a crank handle for starting the engine and a horn to warn other road users.

West Portland Street, seen in 1929 with the shelter on the Esplanade visible in the distance. Apart from the removal of the shelter, little has changed in this view.

Looking northwards along Portland Street at Troon in the early 1920s. On the right is Troon Post Office which had been originally located in Ayr Street before moving to this location. In 1930 it moved again to its current position in Church Street. Visible along the street is the sign for The Picture House cinema and the metal railway bridge near Dodds Garage, carrying the tracks for the Glasgow & South Western Railway Harbour Loop Line which opened in 1892. The bridge was removed in 1973 following the line's closure. Just past the bridge was the Police Station building although this has since closed and the station is now located further north along the street, occupying a new building on the former site of St Meddans House. Also visible on the right is the tall spire of the United Free Church which was built in 1856 on the corner of Portland and Church streets but demolished in 1926 to make way for the new post office building.

Troon Free Church Band of Hope Annual Treat in 1906, with a large group of children dressed in their Sunday best and assembled possibly outside the front of the United Free Church. The church had been established in 1856 and stood on the corner of Portland and Church Street and its tall steeple and clock were a distinctive landmark with the town. Worship stopped in 1914 and the church was finally demolished in 1926 with the clock being removed and used on the steeple of St Meddans Church. The site of the Free Church was later occupied by a number of different shops and in 1932 by the new post office building.

Church Street looking towards the junction with Portland Street in 1938. The Post Office, on the left, was built in 1932 in a chunky neo-classical style from a design by J. Wilson Paterson. Today the building is still used for sorting out mail and deliveries but the branch post office is now across the road, located in the shop called the Pillar Box. Little has changed to the buildings' appearance over the years although the door visible on the left, along with the loading doors and metal hoisting beam above, have now disappeared and a building has also replaced the wall.

Church Street in the early 1950s. The photographer is standing on Academy Street and the unusual gabled building on the left containing all the different shops was built in 1934 from a design by J.B. McInnes. This view has since changed with the building of a modern shop complex directly opposite the Post Office. The visible gap between the buildings on Portland Street has also now been partly developed but retains a traditional Scottish pend-style access through to the rear.

Portland Street in the late 1930s with the junction of Church Street on the left and another of the town's cinemas, the Picture House. In addition to being a newsagent's, White's on the left was also a printer's and agents for the Argosy Circulating Library. Located at the back of the shop, books could be borrowed for a small daily or weekly fee. Argosy is still based in Ireland and at this time had many outlets in various shops across the south west of Scotland.

Looking north along Portland Street in the late 1930s from the Cross, with the metal bridge of the Harbour Loop Line visible in the distance. The railway bridge carried the two tracks which ran from the Troon Junction near the new station and this allowed goods traffic to be transported down to the harbour side. When the bridge was removed in 1973 the large railway embankments that carried the line were also removed and this led to the creation of Jubilee Road and Dukes Road, which follow the course of the line.

An elevated view from the late 1940s taken from the railway bridge of the Troon Harbour Loop Line that was operated by the Glasgow & South Western Railway. On the left is the junction for Church Street. The Picture House opened in 1912 and could seat 850 people but faced stiff competition from the George Cinema which was located just a little further along on the opposite side of the street. Nonetheless it survived until the early 1950s and the building was then occupied by Woolworths until closure in 2009. It is now a Poundland store. Today the premises of White's are occupied by a branch of W.H. Smith.

Portland Street, looking towards the Cross from near the junction with Church Street. c. 1920. In the *New Statistical Account of Scotland* of 1845, Troon was described as being 'neatly built, containing many substantial houses, several handsome cottages for summer residences, and numerous respectable inns and lodging-houses for the accommodation of visitors. A public library is supported by subscription. The post office has a regular delivery by a messenger from the head office of Kilmarnock; two branch banks have been established here, and there is every facility of internal communication.'

Looking westwards along Dundonald Road towards the railway bridge; on the left is the junction of St Meddans Crescent. On 4 February 1898 the worst railway accident in the history of the Glasgow & South Western Railway occurred nearby at the Barassie railway junction. A goods express train from Ayr and a passenger train from Kilmarnock collided at the points leading to the Loop Line and the goods train and its wagons were almost totally destroyed. Seven men from the foot crews were killed and many passengers were injured. An inquiry found the signalman to be partly at fault as he had inadvertently set both engines on their collision course. However, the driver of the goods train (who was also killed) was found to have ignored several danger signals and had actually increased speed towards the junction.

A 1930s view eastwards along Dundonald Road from the railway banking near the junction of Low St Meddans. This road was the principal route from the village to the Cross at Loans and onto Dundonald and also once the main route connecting Troon to Irvine and Ayr. Just visible at the top of the street are the houses at Logan Drive and Wallacefield.

The houses on Logan Drive viewed from the junction with Dundonald Road. This street was one of the main routes for local workers to walk to the large Barassie Carriage and Wagon Works which opened in 1901. The workshops employed 650 people, with more than 300 of them living in Troon, and were later known as the British Railways Engineering Works. They closed in 1972 and the site was later redeveloped for housing. Some of the works' buildings are visible in the distance in this view. The houses on the right stand on Wallacefield Road, named after the farm of Wallacefield that once existed nearby.

Looking southwards in the 1940s along the Main Street towards the Cross at Loans with the war memorial on the left at the junction for the road to Dundonald. This is inscribed with the names of eighteen men who perished in the First World War and six who died in the Second World War. This part of Loans was once very busy and congested as the main A78 road travelled through the centre of the village from Irvine to Ayr following the course of the old turnpike road. Today it is much quieter following the completion of the nearby bypassing dual carriageway.

Looking northwards along Loans Main Street, c. 1915. On the left can be seen the village smiddy with the blacksmith at this time being Mr Tam Fullarton whose family had owned this business for several generations. Further along near the end of the street is the ivy clad walls of the coaching inn dating from the eighteenth century. The shops on the left have now disappeared today to be replaced by a modern petrol garage but the former coaching inn was renovated and transformed in 2009 at a cost of £2 million into the twenty-bedroom Old Loans Inn, a hotel, bar and restaurant.

Looking north along Loans Main Street with the grocer's shop on the left and across the road the gable of the village hall visible on the right behind the wall. The hall opened in 1926, funded by the villagers themselves. It was initially run by volunteers and various trustees before eventually being acquired by the local council in 1969. In 2012 ownership passed back again to the villagers in the form of Loans Community Centre Ltd, the aim of which is to maintain, modernise and upgrade the hall so that it will continue to remain part of the villages' activities for many years to come. Little has changed in this scene today with the buildings still recognisable but modern houses have now been built along Main Street, filling in the gap past the grocer's shop.

Looking north along the Ayr Road towards the village of Loans and the Cross with the wall and entrance to Crossburn House dating from 1832 visible on the right. The hamlet was first mentioned on Blaeu's Atlas of Scotland in 1654 as 'Lons' and then later as 'Lones'; by 1775 it is recorded as Loans. At that time it was merely a cluster of houses straddling the Irvine to Ayr road but by 1832 a toll was in use and two additional roads had been constructed, connecting the village with Dundonald and Troon. In the year 1761 the great smuggling trade had corrupted the entire Ayrshire coast and Loans, being in close vicinity to Troon, was a favourite haunt of the smugglers. Contraband goods such as tobacco, tea, brandy, whisky, foreign rum and occasionally lace and silk were often hidden in vaults below the houses or outside in secret 'brandy-holes' which were located in the surrounding fields. Tales have been recorded of lanterns seen flickering in the dead of night and of often deadly encounters with the government excise men. In modern times the village has steadily increased in size with the building of many modern houses and the creation of new streets all branching off the Main Street.

The new housing scheme built during the inter-war years by the burgh council along the North Shore Road in Barassie. There was a time when only a farm and meal mill existed on the Barassie Burn but in the 1830s a hamlet began to establish itself a mile and a half north of Troon. Later, two Glasgow & South Western Railway lines had their junction here, the Kilmarnock and Troon Branch and the Ayr and Stranraer Branch. A separate railway station was also opened for Barassie and it also got its own eighteen-hole golf course in 1894, the Kilmarnock (Barassie) Golf Club. This led to the building of many fine villas and also what was later known as the Garden Village (houses designed to have plenty of green space around them) and these council houses.

An early 1930s view of Burnfoot Farm and camp site at Barassie, taken from near the railway line. To the left of the farm is the small building that housed the Burnfoot Tea Room, located just off the North Shore Esplanade. It was popular for many years but as Barassie gradually expanded Burnfoot Farm was demolished sometime in the 1950s. The land was used for the building of a new primary school and a large council estate which includes Burnfoot Avenue.

The sandy beach at Barassie in the early 1940s. Just out of view on the right was the Burnfoot Tea Room while in the background is the distinctive Tower Hotel with its restaurant and bar. Built originally as a single-storey villa around 1832–36, it was extended in an Italian design to incorporate a large three-storey tower in 1859 and became a landmark along the Shore Road. It was used as a luxury hotel for many years but it was closed and sold off in 2013, with the building being demolished the following year. Modern flats have now been constructed on the site.

Looking westwards down Hillhouse Road towards the shore from the elevated position of the railway bridge near Barassie train station in the early 1940s. On the right is the junction for Gailes Road. Barassie was once known as the 'New Kilmarnock' when it was founded in the 1830s as a holiday retreat for some of the wealthy businessmen and their families from that town. It was slow to develop at first but soon many fine homes were constructed in what was often later termed the Garden Scheme. This area was located to the north of the Barassie Burn and was known as New Bank Barassie while the area to the south was the Old Bank Barassie. This scene has changed considerably today with a large private residential scheme, Hillhouse Gardens, having been built on the left side of the road.

Barassie Railway Station was opened on 5 August 1839 by the Glasgow, Paisley, Kilmarnock & Ayr Railway. It had two platforms and two lines for the Kilmarnock branch and two platforms and two lines for the adjacent Ayr branch; the branches were connected by a metal footbridge. From 28 October 1850 the Glasgow & South Western Railway operated the route and the station was continually manned until the line was electrified in 1936. Two lines and two platforms still exist on the Ayr branch but the platforms were removed on the Kilmarnock branch after passenger services were withdrawn by British Rail on 3 March 1969. It was reinstated in May 1975 with the Stranraer to London Euston twice-daily service but only one line now remains and all the station buildings have since been demolished. This view looks northwards along the Kilmarnock to Troon lines and visible in the background is the clubhouse of the Kilmarnock Barassie Golf Club which is sandwiched between the two routes.

'Dinner Hour' in a volunteer camp at Lochgreen to the south east of Troon. Little is known as to the actual regiment seen here. Lochgreen took its name from the Reed Loch which was a shallow freshwater loch located on the Fullarton Estate not far from the Southwoods. It was known for many years as the Fullarton House Pond after it was dug out and cleaned of reeds and it was used as a curling pond from the mid-nineteenth century onwards. Popularity in the roaring game had declined by the late 1950s when the loch had become largely overgrown again. It was then drained and the land used for agriculture.

The 2nd Lanarkshire Royal Engineer Volunteers, pictured in 1906 constructing a bridge, trenches and a bomb-proof shelter.

Another view of the men of the 2nd Lanarkshire Royal Engineer Volunteers in 1906.

Men of the 2nd Lanarkshire Royal Engineer Volunteers competing at a sports day around 1912. Various races and competitions were held to test the men's strength, skill, stamina and endurance and, as can be seen in the background here, many locals attended to watch the spectacle. The message on the reverse of this postcard published by J. Stevenson, Troon, reads: 'Dear Aunt Mary, we are having a glorious time. The weather has been splendid and some days it has been too hot. I have been golfing a lot, and bathing nearly every day. There are a great many territorials here, at Irvine Gailes and Ayr. Love from May.' May was staying at a house called 'Janetta' on Welbeck Crescent.

More men of the 2nd pictured outside a thatched hut shelter in 1906.

The 4th Volunteer Battalion Royal Scots and the Border Rifles in camp near Troon, c. 1906. It was during the middle of the nineteenth century that a number of volunteer forces were raised and by 1888 there were seven volunteer battalions, including the 4th, which served alongside the regular infantry units. By 1908 the battalions became the Territorial Force and then later the Special Reserve with many of the soldiers going on to fight in the First World War. The Royal Scots would lose some 11,000 soldiers killed in action with over 40,000 wounded. The men had been mostly recruited from Edinburgh and the surrounding areas into what was the oldest and most senior infantry regiment of the British Army.

A battalion of the Argyll and Sutherland Highlanders in camp near Troon in 1912. It was a common sight around this time to see rows and rows of white tents in the fields surrounding the town as many regulars and volunteers who had recently enlisted were put through their paces at the coast. The regiment had two reserve and five territorial battalions. War was rapidly approaching and many territorial battalions were formed around this time. The Argyll and Sutherland Highlanders were a line infantry regiment and wore the traditional Black Watch tartan kilt with a brown jacket. In this photograph some of the men in the background can be seen wearing kilts.

A military blockhouse built by the Lowland Divisional Engineers (Territorials) at Troon around 1912. A blockhouse was a small fortification, in this case constructed from turf and concrete, with a number of loopholes which allowed its defenders to view and fire in multiple directions if the enemy attacked. The Lowland Divisional Engineers had their headquarters at Rutherglen.

The 156th Scottish Rifles Brigade Camp near Wallacefield, 1913. The brigade was first raised in 1908 when the territorial force was created from the amalgamation of the Yeomanry and the Volunteers. Assigned to the 52nd Lowland Division, this infantry brigade comprised of four volunteer battalions of the Cameronians (Scottish Rifles). It would see active service in both world wars before being disbanded in 1947. Visible in the background of this view are the large chimney and workshop buildings of the Barassie Carriage and Wagon Works operated by the Glasgow & South Western Railway Company.

The 6th Battalion of the Scottish Rifles, or the Cameronians as they were known, at Troon Camp, c. 1908. The men were part of the Territorial Force and can be seen here in the cook house. Many of these volunteers would have been issued a Bible. This was a tradition of joining the regiment and harked back to the original Cameronians, followers of Richard Cameron, the Covenanter leader of the seventeenth century. These men would have travelled through from their barracks at Hamilton to undergo training at the coast.

The 5th Battalion Cameronians (Scottish Rifles) at Wallacefield near Troon, c. 1914. The flat grassy fields at the farm of Wallacefield to the east of Troon, adjacent the railway line, were used regularly at this time for training encampments. The soldiers were part of the Scottish Rifle Brigade, Lowland Division, a territorial force. The men served in France and Flanders from 5 November 1914 until 29 May 1916 when they merged with the 6th Battalion to form the 5/6th Battalion. Some of the men are seen here in full ceremonial uniform, wearing the kilt during a sports day, and the message on the back of the postcard reads: 'Dear Mother, this p.c. was taken before the pipers buglers left to play retreat. James and I managed to reach the finals at the sports, but unfortunately were beaten by other two chaps. There is a good class of sprinter here, and they take a lot of beating.' Marr College now occupies the site of Wallacefield Farm and the Darley Links Golf Course has been formed on the land.

C. Company, 3rd Glasgow Commercial Battalion assembled for parade. The message on the reverse reads: 'To Father from Walter Xmas 1914. Taken at Troon N.B. Nov. 1914. on the Polo Ground.' At the back are some of the newest recruits who are still wearing civilian clothes and who have just enlisted to join the regiment. The Ayrshire Polo Club Ground was located to the south of the Troon Railway Junction and was sandwiched between the loop and main lines off Yorke Road. Today this area of the town has now been developed with the building of many houses but the name is remembered in the streets of Polo Avenue and Polo Gardens.

A group of men possibly from C. Coy., 3rd Glasgow Commercial Battalion of the Highland Light Infantry. Despite there being eleven men in this 1914 postcard, the reverse message names them as 'The Ten Looneys'!

Two men of C. Company 3rd Glasgow Commercial Battalion stand to attention with their rifles at Troon in 1914. The message written on the back of this postcard reads: 'To father from Walter. Taken at Troon Promenade Wed. Oct 20th 1914 – 1.45pm showing England's last hope in full war paint minus the rib ticklers.' The soldiers are pictured on the grassy inshore area off the Esplanade.

Young men, possibly of C. Company, 3rd Glasgow Commercial Battalion of the Highland Light Infantry, practising digging trenches in 1914. Adjacent is the Loop Line of the Glasgow & South Western Railway with one of the signal points visible in the background and one of the bridges on the right carrying a road over the tracks. Beyond the railway line was the flat ground of the Ayrshire Polo Club which means that the men are standing in the vicinity of what is now Darley Crescent. The railway bridge today carries Lochend Road over the tracks.

Men of the C. Coy., 3rd Glasgow Commercial Battalion, pictured in 1914 standing with their rifles on the foreshore area. The message on the reverse of this postcard was from one of the young volunteers and dated 3 November 1914: 'My Dear Mrs Kirk, I intended answering your very kind letter this week but am quite unable as I have a fearfully sore arm the result of vaccination. Half our company is in bed as we got an extra heavy dose. The pain is terrible at times but I hope to be alright soon. Had a 15 mile march yesterday morning and enjoyed it all. Don't expect to be on parade this week …'

More men from C. Coy., 3rd Glasgow Commercial Battalion, assembled together at the entrance to the Unionist Club Buildings at the foot of Templehill in 1914. These men were part-time paid volunteers who had been recruited from the business and trade centres within Glasgow and the surrounding district. They had originally been sent to Gailes before being relocated to Troon to complete their training and some of the men are carrying their Lee-Enfield rifles. These men would shortly have seen action in France.

OLD ESTABLISHED CHURCH, TROON

A group of volunteer soldiers from C. Coy., 3rd Glasgow Commercial Battalion of the Highland Light Infantry, assembled together on Ayr Street opposite Troon Parish Church on the left with the Old Parish Church also visible in the centre. The photograph was taken around 1914 and these volunteers were a familiar sight at the time, marching through the streets or along the Esplanade or on parade in the playground of the Higher Grade School. The soldiers could also be seen running along the sandy beaches to the north and south of the harbour or swimming in the sea as the coast was the perfect place to get them physically fit.

Soldiers of the 17th (Service) Battalion of the Highland Light Infantry pictured in 1914 with their golf clubs on the grassy inshore area just off the Esplanade. Some of the men are sitting on one of the benches and all appear to have their own set of clubs and bag which would have included a driver, a number of irons, a wedge and a putter.

The Higher Grade School was built on Fullarton Street in 1900 to the designs of Robert Ingram and was originally known as Troon Fullarton Public School. It was able to accommodate 800 pupils but the name was changed after an extension was built in 1908 to cater for the increasing numbers who attended. This view shows the clock tower on the west side overlooking the playground and visible on the left is the flag pole that once stood at the corner. The Boys' entrance was below the clock on the west side while the Girls entrance can be seen on the right. A troop of volunteers perhaps from the Glasgow Commercial Battalion of the Highland Light Infantry are marching towards the main entrance where they would turn into the playground and perform their drill. Today the school is still in use but now provides primary education. Secondary pupils now attend Marr College which opened in September 1935.

One of the volunteer battalions, possibly the Argyll and Sutherland Highlanders, on parade in the playground of the Higher Grade School on Fullarton Street in 1914. Troon's flat terrain and long sandy beaches were the perfect location for military training.

Barassie Street, *c.* 1919. The junction with Academy Street is on the right and the Fullarton Street (now Burnside Place) junction is on the left. The railway station is visible in the distance near the end of the street whilst the building on the immediate left surrounded by the wall was formerly a home for nurses but is now used as Barassie Street Health Clinic.

Looking northwards over Troon from the footbridge at the railway station in the early 1920s. On the left are the greenhouses of St Meddans Nursery with the bridge and banking of the Harbour Loop Line in the background along with the spire of the United Free Church. On the far right is the Higher Grade School on Fullarton Street. Originally the train station was located further east, built in 1840 on the edge of the town just to the north of the site of Marr College. It was closed when the new station opened on 2 May 1892. The station was refurbished in the spring of 2004 for the Open Championship that year; it was estimated that about 100,000 extra passengers used the station during the Open week.

Pictured in the late 1920s at Troon Station, ready to head southwards towards Prestwick, Ayr and Stranraer, is a Manson 8 Class 4-4-0 passenger steam locomotive, power Class 1P, which was built in 1895 at Kilmarnock. Originally operated by the Glasgow & South Western Railway as engine No. 15 until 1919, it became No. 401 and then, from 1923 when it ran on the London, Midland & Scottish, it became No. 14179 as seen here. It was scrapped in 1932.

For this view from 1924 the photographer stood on the footbridge spanning the lines at Troon Railway Station. It looks over the houses in Morven Crescent and across Henderson Road and down into Morven Drive, with the council houses on Dundonald Road visible in the distance. On the left is the square tower and small spire of the Roman Catholic Church in Cessnock Road, built in 1911.

Our Lady of the Assumption and Saint Meddan Roman Catholic Chapel stands on Cessnock Road overlooking the junction with St Meddans Street. It was built in 1911 from a design based on late-fifteenth century Scottish architecture, elements of Norman architecture, and incorporating designs from the Holy Rude Church in Stirling. Internally it has an open timber roof incorporating carved angels. The church and adjoining manse were both built from a sum of money left to Troon's Roman Catholic Community by John Patrick Crichton-Stuart, fourth Marquis of Bute.

Golf Crescent and the municipal golf course viewed from one of the houses on Willockston Road with the tennis courts and golf clubhouse visible on the right. In early 1909 a group of 34 golfers formed themselves into the Troon Municipal Golf League. A clubhouse was also built and later in that same year, after the league had been such a resounding success, it was decided to continue under the new name of Troon St Meddans Golf Club. The clubhouse has been enlarged several times over the years and in 1973 a private club named Troon Welbeck Golf Club was also founded. Today both clubs share the clubhouse which was extended again in 2016. There are three challenging eighteen-hole links courses that can be played here – Darley to the north, Fullarton in the centre, and Lochgreen to the south.

Looking down on Golf Crescent from the elevated position of the railway embankment in 1929. In the foreground is the junction for Victoria Drive while the road to the train station is on the left. The municipal tennis courts and pavilion are visible while on the extreme left is an artillery gun dating from the First World War which stood alongside two others in front of the municipal golf course clubhouse. Below the guns are some of the wooden sheds that were used by professionals who practised and taught their craft on the course.

The municipal tennis courts and pavilion pictured in the late 1920s with the municipal golf course clubhouse visible in the background and the railway station on the left. To the right of the clubhouse can be seen the starter's box and the large semi-detached villas on Harling Drive. There were four municipal tennis courts and while they no longer exist, the sport is still played in the town at nearby Troon Lawn Tennis Club.

Flooding at the Cross around 1930. On the right are the premises of Welsh the grocer. Note the small white sign on the corner above the shop window which carries the message, 'Premises for Sale'. The premises were indeed sold and later became a Granada TV rental shop and are now the premises of a branch of Coral bookmakers. In the centre of this view is the distinctive domed entrance to The Pavilion cinema at No. 15 Templehill, which opened in 1920. It could cater for 800 people, later increased to 850. It closed down sometime in the 1950s and was later demolished; Brodlie's chemist now occupies the site.

A view from the Cross looking into Ayr Street, March 1924. Although the Cross was one of the busiest areas in the town men could still stand to chat in the middle of the street, unimaginable today at this often congested junction.

Ayr Street, c. 1910. The circular sign on the left informs road users that the maximum permitted speed is '10 Miles Per Hour' and this would have applied to all road users, including those on cycles and horse-drawn vehicles.

A 1904 photograph of Ayr Street with the old parish church from 1837 on the left. Previously the congregation had used a building on Barassie Street since 1822 while the church seen here was itself superseded by the new parish church in 1895 (the old church became the parish church hall). On the right the attractive red sandstone buildings were designed by James Hay and built in 1900. As the shops faced directly west they would often have their blinds down to shade the shop frontage from the glare of the sun on fine days.

Looking south west down St Meddans Street towards the South Beach in the early 1930s. The photographer has an elevated position standing on the banking near the road bridge of the Glasgow & South Western Railway Troon Harbour Loop Line. Visible on the right at the junction of Church Street is St Meddans Church, built in 1888, while across the road at the junction of Bentinck Drive is the corner tower of the Mar Lodge Hotel which has since become several private residences.

Looking southwards along Bentinck Drive in the early 1900s with the wall of the Mar Lodge Hotel (later known as the Bentinck Hotel) visible on the right. Bentinck Drive is named after the man who was solely responsible for transforming the hamlet of Troon into the vibrant coastal town it has become today: William Henry Bentinck, fourth Duke of Portland and also Marquis of Titchfield. It was his vision and wealth that was responsible for building and developing the harbour from 1808 onwards and also the railway from Kilmarnock to Troon that was responsible for so much of the harbour's business.

Bentinck Drive in the late 1930s, looking northwards with the photographer standing adjacent the Bowling Green which is just out of view on the left, followed by the turreted house standing at the junction for Dallas Road. Further along on the left of the street is the Mar Lodge Hotel followed by the towering spire of St Meddans Church, built in 1888 on Church Street. Also visible in the distance is the spire of the United Free Church.

The tennis courts of the Lawn Tennis Club and bowling green pictured in March 1924 with the houses on Dallas Road and Bentinck Drive visible in the background along with the tall spire of St Meddans Church on Church Street. The tennis courts were originally laid out in 1892, paid for by Sir Alexander Walker who also provided funds to build a small clubhouse containing two large changing rooms, toilets, a small kitchen area and a veranda. Troon Lawn Tennis Club was officially formed in 1895 and was originally known as Troon Lawn Tennis and Croquet Club. For many years the club used only grass courts but in recent years these were replaced by artificial surfaces which are also floodlit at night to allow play during the winter.

![Bowling Green and Tennis Courts, Troon]

The bowling green and tennis courts off Bentinck Drive in the early 1950s, pictured from one of the houses on Dallas Street. On the right is the corner of the bowling club pavilion followed by the flag staff and then the smaller clubhouse of the lawn tennis club. The houses on Victoria Drive are visible in the background. Troon Bowling Club was established in 1840 and initially played on a green located near the new parish church. Membership steadily increased and as a result it moved to its present location in 1897. The Duke of Portland made the land available adjacent to a new tennis club and the greens were ready for play the following year. As can be seen in this photograph, there are two playing greens with ten rinks and a clubhouse, which has since been extended.

South Beach Hotel dates from around the 1890s and was originally built as two separate semi-detached houses which were later merged to create the hotel. The hotel is still in business today.

A 1970s view of the Craiglea Hotel located on the South Beach with the signs advertising that it was open to non-residents and that it was also fully licensed. As Troon developed into a popular summer resort many large villas were converted into luxury hotels, including the South Beach Hotel, the Craiglea Hotel, Welbeck Hotel, Mar Lodge Hotel (later known as the Bentinck Hotel), the Suncourt Hotel, the Towers Hotel (Barassie) and also the Piersland Lodge Hotel. The latter was built on Craigend Road in 1899 in a mock-Tudor style and was for many years the luxury home of Sir Alexander Walker, the grandson of Johnnie Walker, who founded the famous Kilmarnock-based Scotch whisky blenders. The Craiglea Hotel has since closed and been converted into a number of private residences.

An elevated view from 1920s, looking north along the South Beach from the veranda of a villa near the junction of Lochend Road. On the left is one of the shelters on the Esplanade. In the centre near the spire of St Meddans Church can be seen the gasometer of the gas works which was located near the bottom of Barassie Street, overlooking the Pan Rocks. Adjacent the gas works was the slaughter house. The site is now occupied by the local authority recycling centre and a small car park.

Troon Golf Club clubhouse pictured in the early 1900s with the Marine Hotel in the background. A golfer is preparing to tee off on the first tee whilst on the right is the small starter's box. Troon Golf Club was officially formed on 16 March 1878 by a few golfing enthusiasts who had met in the nearby Portland Arms Hotel. A five-hole course was laid out on the lands of Craigend Farm and this was extended to twelve holes in 1883 and to eighteen in 1886. A new clubhouse was also built around this time and the links course was designed by George Strath and later improved by Willie Fernie who was responsible for the famous Postage Stamp and Railway holes. Two major extensions were also added to the clubhouse and to mark its centenary in 1978 the club was awarded Royal status; now known as Royal Troon Golf Club, it provides one of the most challenging links courses in the world. In July 2016 Royal Troon Golf Club held The 145th Open Championship and the famous Claret Jug was won by the Swede Henrik Stenson. This was the ninth time The Open has been held at Troon.

The Portland Golf Club clubhouse and course with a golfer at the first hole in the early 1920s. The Portland links course was designed by Troon professional golfer William Fernie, winner of the Open Championship in 1883, and was opened in 1895 on land that had been purchased from the Duke of Portland. Originally it was named the Relief Course for the nearby Championship Course (relief in the sense that it was not as difficult as the Championship Course and offered golfers another course to play when the Championship Course was busy). The clubhouse was just a small pavilion or white hut but when the course was redesigned in the early 1920s by Dr Alister MacKenzie a new much larger clubhouse was built. At this time the course was renamed the Portland Course. In the background on the right is the Marine Hotel dating from 1895 with the staff quarters and the Marine and Bogend Garage in the foreground on Crosbie Road; on the left in the distance is the Ladies' clubhouse. Today the Portland clubhouse still stands on Crosbie Road but in the background the former garage and staff quarters for the Marine Hotel have now been converted into a restaurant and health and leisure centre. The first hole is still in exactly the same spot and is named Danderin' Inn after the Shepherd's Cottage that once stood close by.

Pictured in the early 1900s is the putting green at Lochgreen which formed part of Troon Municipal Golf Course while in the background is the thatched Shepherd's Cottage that stood at Bogend on the Fullarton Road. As the 'Danderin' Inn, this was once a favourite haunt of smugglers.

The Ladies Golf Club at Troon was founded in 1882 although women had been playing on the Championship Course for several years prior to this. On the left of this view is the Ladies Golf Club clubhouse on the Portland Course. It was built on Crosbie Road on land purchased from the Duke of Portland and was officially opened on 11 September 1897. Since 1973 the Helen Holm Scottish Stroke Play Championship has been hosted by the club with both the Portland and the Championship courses used during the three-day competition. Today the clubhouse is little changed with only the disappearance of the chimneys and first floor veranda.

Pictured around 1910, this row of thatched cottages were known as the Old Row. Owned by the Fullarton Estate and used by the workers, they were located on the unusually named Isle O' Pin's Road which led up to Fullarton House. The name is believed to have derived from the four large pillars, or pins, that once stood at the entrance gates to the house. Before being called Old Row the cottages were known as Old Causeyside and were eventually demolished.

Heather House, located close to the ruins of Crosbie Kirk, was the attractive gate house to Fullarton House. The entrance gates to the estate stood out of picture on the left. The cottage was destroyed by a fire in March 1958.

Fullarton House was built by William Fullarton in 1745 within the extensive grounds of the Fullarton Estate to the east of Troon. In 1772 a large stable block designed by the Adam brothers was added by his son, Colonel William Fullarton. The Fullarton line of possession came to an end in 1805 when the house and estate were purchased by William Bentinck, fourth Duke of Portland, to become his main residence while he developed the harbour area and his railway. In 1928 the house was purchased by Troon Town Council and converted into a number of private flats. By the 1960s the building required extensive modernisation and restoration which was estimated to be too costly and as a result it was demolished in 1966. The stable block was subsequently converted into a number of private flats in 1974. The site of the actual house is now a car park for Fullarton Public Park and picnic area and all that remains are the two large stone pediments visible on the corners of this photograph from the early 1920s.

The North Wing of Fullarton House and its beautiful stained glass window, with the front of the house on the right, viewed in the 1920s. Notable guests who stayed within its walls are believed to have included Prince Louis Napoleon Bonaparte (later Emperor Napoleon III), while he attended the Eglinton Tournament in 1839, and also Robert Burns. When the house was purchased by the Duke of Portland in 1805 its frontage faced eastwards but it was considerably altered so the back became the front to take advantage of the panoramic views overlooking Troon and the Firth of Clyde.

A chapel was first built at Crosbie in 1229 but the present church dates from 1691 when it formed part of the extensive Fullarton Estate and was surrounded by a small village. It is recorded that the roof was blown off and the gable end damaged during a terrible storm in 1759 which happened to occur on the same day Robert Burns was born in Alloway. The ancient chapel was never repaired as it was hardly used at the time and it was left roofless. The kirkyard is surrounded by a small wall and contains the seventeenth-century grave of David Hamilton of Bothwellhaugh who was the alleged assassin of the Earl of Moray. The kirkyard was the burial place for Troon up until 1862 but today the old Kirk of Crosbie is surrounded by trees and stands at the side of the road to Monkton, accessed via the Wrack Road, or the Smuggler's Trail as it is known today, which runs past the church west through the South Woods, over the railway line, and across the Championship Course to the shore.

Alton Dairy was located approximately two miles south of Troon within the South Woods area and is pictured here around 1905. The view is looking northwards along the Southwood Road and just past the dairy round the corner is the junction for the Monktonhill Road. Little remains of the dairy apart from a couple of derelict buildings which have recently been put up for sale as a development opportunity. Part of the dairy site has also been taken up by a row of modern cottages. On the left of this view, where the children can be seen, is the location of the lavish Frognal Mansion House and its 32-acre estate. The house was constructed in 1909 for a wealthy Indian tea planter and it was later used as an elderly persons' home before being bought in 2003 and extensively restored by chef and hotelier Bill Costley who used it for a time as an exclusive hotel and restaurant and later as his personal home. It was sold in 2014 for £3.5 million to Britain's biggest lottery winners, Colin and Christine Weir, who won £161 million on the EuroMillions lottery.

HMS *Orion* was a Leander-class light cruiser which served with distinction in the Royal Navy during the Second World War. Launched on 24 November 1932, her crew of 680 were protected by four 102mm forward guns, eight six-inch naval guns, twelve machine guns and eight torpedo tubes. In addition, she also carried a catapult-launched Fairey Seafox aircraft, later replaced with a Supermarine Walrus. The vessel served extensively in the Mediterranean and received thirteen battle honours; she also carried the ashes of former Governor General of Canada and author of *The Thirty-Nine Steps*, John Buchan, back to England for burial in February 1940. *Orion* ended her service in 1947 and was sold for scrap in July 1949 to the British Iron and Steel Corporation; she is seen here being broken up that year.

HMS *Anthony* was an A-class destroyer of the Royal Navy that served extensively during the Second World War. The vessel was commissioned into service on 14 February 1930 and was built by the Scotts Shipbuilding and Engineering Co. in Greenock. Armed with four 120mm guns, two single two-pounder anti-aircraft guns, eight 21-inch torpedo tubes and six depth charges, her motto was *Portia in Arduia*: 'brave under difficulties'. The destroyer was responsible for evacuating 3,000 men from Dunkirk and in 1942 was involved in Operation Ironclad at Diego Suarez where she landed fifty marines ashore to break the Vichy French defences, resulting in the surrender of the port. By 1945 she had been converted into an air target ship and was also used for damage control trials before later being placed in reserve. HMS *Anthony* was sold for scrap in February 1948 to the British Iron and Steel Corporation and is seen here at their breaking yard at Troon in July of that year. Part of her upper structure had been cut away by this point.

HMS *Eskimo* was a Tribal-class destroyer operated by the Royal Navy throughout the Second World War, having been commissioned into service on 30 December 1938. The vessel was hit by a torpedo fired from a German destroyer during the Second Battle of Narvik in April 1940. The massive explosion resulted in the destroyer losing her bow but after temporary repairs she eventually managed to return to Newcastle to be rebuilt. HMS *Eskimo* was again badly damaged by German dive bombers while in action in the Mediterranean and in 1944 she, along with a Canadian destroyer and a Czech liberator aircraft, sank a German U-boat in the English Channel. Following the war the destroyer was used for some time as a headquarters and accommodation ship before finally being used as a target ship at Gareloch. This photograph, taken from the bridge of HMS *Javelin*, looks down on the structure of HMS *Eskimo* in September 1949 as she was broken up at the British Iron and Steel Corporation's yard at Troon.

HMS *Furious* was a modified Courageous-class battle cruiser built for the Royal Navy during the First World War. Launched on 15 August 1916, the battle cruiser was lightly armoured with only two heavy eighteen-inch guns, one forward and one aft. *Furious* was reclassified as an aircraft carrier in September 1925 after being reconstructed with a full length flight deck. She had a crew of 795 personnel, could carry 36 aircraft, and was over 786 feet in length. Used extensively for training and testing of naval aircraft and for ferrying RAF aircraft, in 1944 *Furious* also played a role in a number of attacks on the German battleship *Tirpitz*. By April 1945 the aircraft carrier was decommissioned from service and was sold for scrap in 1948 to the British Iron and Steel Corporation. Her hulk is seen here in November 1949 being broken up in their yard at Troon. The large flight deck and all of her upper structure had been removed before the hulk was towed down from Dalmuir, and by 1954 she had been completely broken up. In the background of this view are the gas works and the council houses along the North Shore Road.

Another image of HMS *Furious* being broken up for scrap in November 1949 at the British Iron and Steel Corporation yard in Troon. This photograph shows the vessel's hulk which appears to have been beached onto the shoreline area near the East Breakwater and broken up into sections.

Looking east along Templehill towards the Cross in 1979, with the premises of the 'Aubergine' shoe shop on the left while across the road a delivery is underway at the Allway Foods store at No. 65. This is now the premises of Cowans Baby Centre and the former shoe shop is now occupied by Rentolease, an estate and letting agents.

Looking northeast along Portland Street from the Cross in the early 1980s. Towards the right of the view the Tennent's Lager sign marks the Lonsdale Bar which was established in 1894 at No. 15. Further down is the distinctive cloud-shaped cream tile entrance of the George Cinema. Capable of seating over 1,200 patrons, it was designed by James McKissack and opened in 1937 as the Embassy Cinema by the K.R. Blair Circuit. It was taken over by the George Palmer Circuit in 1946 and renamed the George. Closing in 1974, the cinema lay derelict for many years before it was finally demolished to make way for flats in 1986/87. The shops either side of the location of the cinema entrance still have cream tiles.

Another 1970s view, this time looking from West Portland Street into Portland Street. Today little has changed apart from the disappearance of the ugly metal railings. The shoe shop on the right still trades today under the name of Camerons.

A similar view from the late 1970s. Little has changed since with only the shop premises containing different businesses, although Charles Duncan's butcher's, established in 1920 at No. 15 Ayr Street, is still going strong today.

Ayr Street, pictured around 1978 looking north towards the busy Cross and the Bank of Scotland building at the foot of Templehill.

A 1980s' view of Ayr Street with the parish church on the left. One of Troon's best known sons was former Scotland and British Lions rugby player Gordon Brown. Affectionately known by many as 'Broon frae Troon', he was born in one of the local council estates in 1947, son of former Scotland goalkeeper Jock Brown. He was capped thirty times at international level for Scotland and also played in eight tour test matches for the British Lions. Following retirement he became a regular guest speaker and commentator for ITV and covered both the 1991 and 1995 World Cup tournaments. Gordon also worked tirelessly for charity but sadly passed away from cancer in 2001 at the age of only 53. Many famous personalities and sportsmen from the world of sport attended the funeral at the parish church and a commemorative garden was also later created in the vicinity of the nearby library to honour his memory.